Stories & Poems

of a

Gullah Native

Elijah Heyward, Jr.

ISBN-10: 1-937705080
ISBN-13: 978-1-9377050-8-4
Also available in E-book:
ISBN-13: 978-1-9377050-9-1

Library of Congress Control Number: 2012952661
Printed in the United States of America

𝓜

MavLit Publishing, LLC
www.maverick-books.com
P. O. Box 1103
Irmo, S.C. 29063

Cover Design: Maverick Literary
Cover Photo: Getty Images

To
Elijah Heyward, Sr. and Ethel Cohen Heyward

Stories & Poems

of a

Gullah Native

Elijah Heyward, Jr.

Contents

Introduction

While experimenting with jingles in the classroom, I would write historical verses on African-Americans. These poems were my tribute to trailblazers of the best the human spirit can achieve.

Harriet Tubman, Frederick Douglass, and Rosa Parks were some of the individuals of note in which I tried to capture their life contributions.

These poems were also my attempt at breaking the jingle syndrome. My students appreciated the new material and they eagerly looked for the next personality or historical event to be put into verse. My students also gave grades to each poem.

During the month of February, I presented each student an original poem as my contribution to African-American History Month. We called it our "Black History Moment."

These poems are a sincere effort at living up to my kiddies' expectations while hopefully presenting them with positive examples of achievement—and of course some fun.

The Farm

Every summer that I can recall, I worked on a farm until I reached legal employment age. Working on a farm picking tomatoes and cucumbers along with other tasks provided me money to buy school clothes as well as financial support for my family.

Work on the farm started early before the sun got hot. A bus of the old public school variety would pick us up and carry us out to the field. The foreman, who was usually a light-skinned black male, would assign us rows to be picked.

Because the rows were so long, a tractor would cut across the rows to shorten the distance of carrying buckets loaded with fresh picked cucumbers or green tomatoes. Boxes would be positioned at the beginning and throughout the long rows to receive the fresh pickings. We earned thirty cents for each box that was completely filled.

At lunchtime, everyone found some type of shade from the sun's rays. Usually, it was an oak tree or gathering in or around the bus. Lunch consisted of a honey bun, a lunchmeat sandwich, and a Dixie Cola. We usually brought it out to the field with us because once we got there we did not leave until the sun went down.

Wake up to pack a lunch of meat,
Dixie Cola, honey bun, a real treat.

Ride long buses to the farm,
Early in the morning, everything calm.

The language flavorful and full of joy,
No one around to disrespect or call you boy.

Colorful clothes practical and neat,
Must be worn to beat the heat.

Long rows of green, an endless task,
The quicker you pick, more money made fast.

Back-breaking labor with dignity and pride,
No complaints, all taken in stride.

Oak

This tree has seen it all
Since the beginning of my people
A sprig planted by mandated labor
And watered with the tears of many

It grew strong and proud
Encircled by rings of constant travail
Witness to the journey of forgotten souls
Only if the truth could be told

Stately, imposing, dignified
Limbs reach out to the Heavens
A rope dangles with alarm
Shadows embodies a spiritual calm

County

Boy, my life has changed,
Everything has been re-arranged.
I can't raise my hog,
Nor can I have a dog.

My hog pen, an unsightly mess,
But my food nonetheless.
The county has big plans, you see,
And none of them include me.

The last I hear, I can't say,
Progress is moving fast my way.
My care-free life is fraught with woe,
Can't pay my taxes; where will I go?

The Job

Go to work,
Treated like a jerk.
Don't expect to have a brain,
But work just the same.

The job, it's a must,
So we never fuss.
The pay ain't great,
So, some days we're late.

We gather for lunch,
We enjoy that bunch.
We laugh, we're in tune,
Lunch ends too soon.

The day wears on; it's a waste,
We can't wait to leave this place.
If the boss only knew this fact,
One day we ain't coming back.

Week

I work hard for the man,
He doesn't like me, anyway,
So when he turns his back I play.

For my lady and I,
To get bucks from the boss,
This job is my only source.

Monday through Thursday stuck,
Stick to the grind.
But Friday is my lady and mine.

Saturday we shop
With hard-earned cash,
It's late in the night before we crash.

Early on Sunday,
We're off to church to pray,
God has given us another Monday.

Directions

———————————

Where can I find Uncle Billy Bob?
I'm his first cousin, Rob.
I'm here from New York,
I don't have a car so I walk.

Go down the dirt road,
Along side the cornfield,
You'll see the dog house in the backyard.
Go behind the big oak,
Up the steps,
Through the screen door.

Is that very far?
Remember, I don't have a car.
You know in the city I would take a bus.
I don't mean to argue; don't mean to fuss.

Go down the dirt road,
Along side the cornfield,
You'll see the dog house in the backyard.
Go behind the big oak,
Up the steps,
Through the screen door.

Point me in the right direction again—
Just follow that road around the bend.
You'll see Uncle Billy Bob in the den.
Knock on the door and step back a bit.
He must see you or he'll have a fit

So, down the dirt road,
Along side the cornfield,
You'll see the dog house in the backyard.
Go behind the big oak,
Up the steps,
Through the screen door.

I followed your directions, and it's odd
It seems we've been standing in the backyard.

Colored Restroom

W̲hen I was about six, maybe seven, my father and I went to a service station. He was driving a 1956 yellow and black Oldsmobile. I would ride in the back seat right behind my father. He always insisted on having four doors because he didn't like bending over to let someone over into the rear seat.

Just like almost every other black person in Beaufort, South Carolina, we stopped at the same service station. I believe the "service" there was bearable. You have to understand in the early 1960s being a black person in the South was challenging. So, finding places to get "service" was not always easy. But at this station, the climate was pleasant.

We had stopped to make small talk with friends and buy gas. I wanted to go to the restroom, so I asked my father for permission. He said, "Yes, it's around back." I knew even at that age that meant there were two restrooms: one for Colored and the other White, and you did not go into the "White Only" rest room.

I walked around back to the Colored restroom. The doorknob was missing, and a tree limb was hanging in the door. The outside of the door was white, but it was dirty. As I pushed the door to enter, the place was messy and unsanitary; it appeared that it had never been cleaned. The outside seemed more available than the facilities inside.

I ran back to my father and asked him about the differences in the two restrooms. He acknowledged by question, but did not respond. His facial expression was of deep concern. I merely got back into the car and we drove off.

I sure could go to the restroom, Dad
I've got to go; I've got to go bad!
Son, the restrooms are out back,
Colored, carry your brother, Jack

Dad, I'm too young to read,
Do you think they care?
I've got to go bad!

Son, your restroom is out back,
Colored, many things it lack.
It's usually dirty and unclean,
The way we're treated is very mean.

Now, go and relieve yourself quick.
This system we practice is sick.
"Whites Only" are the signs we see,
Most believe, but why should it be?

Son, the restroom is out back,
"Colored Only," it's out back.

Would You Want to Be Black Like Me?

Let me teach a lesson of strife
I'm not treated very nice
Maybe it's a color thing
But rejection and frustration it surely brings.

At this place I stand in line
But they refuse to serve my kind
I object and begin to tell
How they don't treat me very well

Some would say you're all the same
Complaining but never taking the blame
Everyone's life has been up hill a bit
Get up and move, don't just stand or sit

Change the color of your skin
That's a good place to begin
It's a shame it wouldn't last
You'll always be second class.

System

Consider it a privilege to be here
We're civilized, it's true
We'll take care of you.

Rights, you have none
Don't bother to run away
On this plantation you will stay

Your work is menial
You get living quarters, too
Continue to work; we'll take care of you

Come to the back door
Look at the ground
Do this and we'll keep you around

We'll take care of you
That's what we'll do!

Journey

Taken from home, anyway they can
Chained, beaten, treated less than a man
Endured a journey across tumultuous seas
Bent but not broken stayed on our knees

Enslaved to work from sun up to sun down
Only to enrich the southern ground
Set free, though still in chains
Never envisioned having a brain

Threatened by men in white
Not even allowed to put up a fight
Separate but equal established as a rule
At their mercy a useless tool

Fought in wars, died, too
No respect, still nothing to do
Demanded civil rights
Marches, protests, a great fight
Gains were made for some
For the masses never to come!

Middle Passage

Snatched from your homeland
Becoming a part of another's plan
Disoriented, bewildered, emotions soaring
Reassured by God every morning

Stacked deep in the hole
Thought to be without a soul
Leg irons adorn every row
Sorrow and grief a constant foe

Nature unforgiving tossed about
Little, if ever, allowed out
Night and day passed as such
We owe God so very much

The strain of the voyage took its toll
The crew repented, so I've been told
"Amazing Grace" the redemptive song
Thank God, Almighty, we're still around!

Plantation

Our bondsmen were happy
They laugh, sing, and enjoy life
Northerners say an existence in strife
They are fed, housed, and cared for
Excellent conditions leave us alone

Did anybody ask them
About their servitude?
Would they agree everything is smooth?
I guess the whip and the lash
Are accepted, leave us alone!

Women work in the system, too
Duties the same, additional task
Having many children, and fast—
It's just a part of the economics
Good business, leave us alone!

The plantation gentle and kind
Only in the owner's mind
Those who work without any hope
Kept their silence trying to cope
Everything going fine, leave us alone!

Plantation Thoughts

It's something in a name,
Some sure believe that.
Things can't be as it once was,
But perceptions last just because.

Slavery is gone,
Maybe that's true.
Though behind that gate,
You better not be late.

Work holds dignity,
A bit of self-respect.
Centuries have passed, what is wrong?
Seems nothing has changed in this old town!

I Trust In

The white man's ice is colder,
A reality the African-American still shoulder.
My people of color and race,
Mentally still kept in their place.

The simple things to help ourselves,
We leave to someone else.
But God says through Him all things are possible,
The way they think is incorrigible.

White approval we seek,
Only to make ourselves weak.
We only believe white is right,
Never trusting in God's holy might.

A great people wandered away,
Dominated by whites even to this day.
Whites rescue their own,
African-American thought must be reborn!

It's a Shame

Scare them, burn crosses,
Let's show them we're the bosses.
Break that spiritual bond,
Burn that church to the ground.

The angry, do they sleep?
Can hate run so deep?
These actions cannot win,
Remember God judges sin.

What a League

Let's play ball.
Come one and all.
No whites would let us in,
No one thought it sin.

We barn stormed
We never stayed home
Cars, buses, we traveled far,
We hoped of becoming a star.

We were big among our folks.
We played for peanuts, quite broke.
Leagues formed, what a start—
Whites thought we were getting too smart.

Games were played against white teams.
We did too well now it seems.
Our best and brightest taken away,
Nothing left, it's sad I'll say.

High Finance

Minorities can't handle the big accounts.
Stick with what you know,
We're bringing you along slow.

Financial world a closed market.
The bastion of wealth,
Ready to admit no one else.

A closed market's for the chosen few.
Their methods make business skyrocket,
Accept investments from anybody's pocket.

Capital rules in this arena.
All we care about is the bottom line,
Sorry, if you're not our kind.

Transportation, Please

Yes, I want to rent a car.
No, I won't take it far.
Can my request be met?
No, we refuse, our rules are set.

I have a credit card,
It's over the limit, but I work hard.
Is there a chance I could use another?
No way, don't even bother.

I rented this vehicle at your sister store,
Now I need two vehicles more.
Everything is in order, I called ahead.
Sorry, I don't care what they said.

We have been given the run around.
Seems we're hearing the same old song.
Work hard, gain their respect,
Looks like they're not ready yet.

I Feel a Poem Coming On

I was sitting in church one Sunday observing the different expressions of faith. Everything was taking its usual course. The preacher was standing stately in the pulpit. The deacons were seated to the preacher's left, church mothers and deaconesses to the right, the choir behind him, and the righteous brothers and sisters in front of him.

The ushers roamed the sanctuary ready to issue fans to assist the emotionally overwhelmed. When not on duty, they occupied the last row of pews on both sides of the church. Duty brothers and sisters stood erect and poised to answer any disturbances out of the ordinary. Their mission was clear, jubilation was fine, but kept within the framework of the service.

The stage was set for some great performances. The African-American church service that I observed was unfolding into scenes of righteous humor.

The choir sang an emotionally charged gospel tune. But one, maybe two of the members, had missed their calling. So they began sing for the Lord mostly out of tune. The parade of friends, family, and visitors resembled a fashion show with the center aisle as their runway.

The pastor now launched into a highly-charged sermon, his voice resonated throughout. His spirit seemed to have struck an emotional chord with the congregation, causing some to jump and shake uncontrollably.

The deacons, a sedate bunch, sat supporting the pastor's effort with a constant chorus of 'Amen"—at least for those still coherent. That's because the comfort of the pews and controlled climate had softly taken some into REM sleep.

With the sermon coming to completion, the pastor descends from the pulpit with an invitation to the lost to join the fellowship of believers. The church stands while those who desire prayer move forward, bringing their burdens to the Lord. The choir now sings almost in a whisper as the pastor makes petition to the Lord. It is a moment of deep conviction, sincerity, and solemnity.

Afterward, the chairman of the deacons motions to the trustees to help support the work of the Lord. The trustees, while the choir sings of course, direct those in an orderly manner to the table of capitalism. No service is complete without the custom of asking for send-by money.

The brothers and sisters strut toward the front to once again display the latest fashion statement. With the entire fanfare over, the trustees disappear into a back room to count the funds given by the "least among us."

The service ends with a final praise to the Almighty with shouts and hands raised, acknowledging their dependence and oneness. I look around to see if anyone other than I had enjoyed the theater of this church service.

If no church on Sunday,
What would we talk about on Monday?

Sister had on this dress,
She pranced without rest.

25

Brother had on this new suit,
On this he must have spent all of his loot.
Sister clapping a constant sway,
Sure hope she doesn't fall this way!

If no church on Sunday,
What would we talk about on Monday?

That sister's child cried and yelled,
What the pastor said no one could tell.
Most of the deacons taking a nap,
Bible and programs in their lap.
Sister sang this song all out of tune,
Oh, how we wish she'd get lessons soon.

If no church on Sunday,
What would we talk about on Monday?

The trustee took up the offering to count,
We'll never know the right amount.
So and so ushered all in white,
I heard he'd been out drinking all last night.
The sick need attention, the hungry yet to feed,
I wish someone would take the lead!

If no church on Sunday,
What would we talk about on Monday?

Lesson

Bible study, a few show up
Information directly from the Lord's cup.

One hour, a most righteous time
The dedicated few don't seem to mind.

A spiritual exchange of scriptural truth
The mind is expanded, gray matter shaken loose.

The revelation of God free to all
Most refuse to answer the call.

Pride

You'll never drink from my cup,
You'll never measure up.
Stand up, look at me,
Special like me you'll never be.

Bigness, all puffed up, I'm great,
My reflection even comes late.
Standard procedure to be in control,
Forcing others to play a role.

Surely, it's no big deal—
Ego, it's not real.
Funny all the things you had,
Has only made you sad.

Love

Is it a thing of thought,
Or can it be bought?
Maybe it's a gift of flowers
That only last for a few hours.

Though it's always true,
Love continually confuses you.
Days of joyous glee,
Months of can this ever be?

Love constantly reveals to all,
Time after time as we fall.
But we rise to regain our soul,
Love never loses its hold.

Let God Talk

It's lightning outside,
Rain dancing on the roof.
We are all in the closet,
That's the absolute truth.

Sweat dropping like marbles,
Clustered like sardines in a can.

God must be talking,
That's what the old folks say.
I sure hope God isn't long winded,
It's hot in here today!

Economics

Does God want us poor?
Must be a lie for sure.
Churches preach heaven and hell,
Economics a much tougher sell.

Booker T. taught industry, a simple plan.
Heaven sent to the new freed man.
Marcus taught pride and wealth.
Our people wanted something else.

Religion adapted quite well.
Sermons continued; the masses fell.
Our spiritual leaders helped us cope.
The world to come offered great hope.

Now the picture is bleak.
Economic security, we still seek.
Hundreds of years speaking to God.
All we did was settle for a job.

It's Sad

You want to go broke?
Build a business depending on black folk.
Jealousy, envy, hate,
They'll do whatever it take.

They'll support you,
You're their kind,
You never know what's on their mind.

Depending on black folk,
One thing for sure, it's a given,
You're never gonna make a livin'.

Wait

Patience, could I get some?
Anybody got any to spare?
Never had much,
Is there a thing as such?

Let's bet you can't stand another minute,
On the edge, you've reached your limit.
Relax, just wait, and don't be in a hurry,
But that's part that makes me worry!

Student View

Why bother me with education?
I know what I need,
Quick money, capitalistic greed.

Why rack your brain?
Trying to teach,
We never listen; it doesn't reach.

Man, you're stressed.
Why should you care?
Money and education not even a pair.

Fast bucks, the good life,
We see it everywhere,
The schoolhouse, we'll never get it here.

Burn Out

I've got to shout,
Please let me out.
No one to teach,
Most times I preach.
They know it all,
Setting up for a fall.

Pressure from the top,
Don't give up; don't stop.
Parents give no support,
It's so hard to cope.
It seems a hopeless case,
Let me out of this place!

Lord

You said ask and it shall be given
This life is not livin'
What's going on?
I feel so all alone.
Victory is mine, so it's said,
But I much rather go back to bed.

Stand at the Egg Farm

In our community, everyone knew each other and the bonds were close. Families extended beyond your house, and last name didn't matter. It could be compared to the concept of a village where everyone worked for the benefit of the whole. In hindsight, maybe we got along well because we shared in the same struggle.

It seemed that everyone at one time during his or her teen years worked at the local egg farm. I can remember my first hourly wage—thirty-five cents. The jobs on the egg farm varied, but all involved maintenance of chickens: de-beaking, vaccinating, collecting eggs, and capture for market were some of the activities.

The work was long, hard, and dusty. Each house had a capacity of thousands, and the lights never went off at night. I often thought that chickens must have been the dumbest birds on earth because as long as the lights were on they laid eggs.

The owner really took advantage of this situation. The chickens would fight and injure each other with their sharp beaks, so they had to be de-beaked. The process of de-beaking a chicken was pretty straight-forward. Coral the chicken in groups of about one hundred, capture them one by one, and hand it to a person operating the de-beaking machine. The machine was a tripod with a guillotine-like apparatus on top. Instead of a blade, there was a hot piece of metal.

The chicken was held by its feet. Its beak was guillotined off then pressed upon the hot metal and burned off. Then the wound would be cauterized, one chicken at a time, all day long, eight houses, thousands of chickens, at thirty-five cents an hour.

After working, we would stop at Freddie's store and buy our favorite meal of a Coke for fifteen cents and a honey bun for a dime. Then we would sit under the big oak tree nearby and eat.

On one occasion, the owner shorted me by two dollars. The rest of the crew had received six dollars for their work; I received only four. All of us had done the same job. We worked the same hours. But all of us didn't receive the same pay. The foreman expressed his disbelief, but only to me. He promised to plead my case the next time they worked.

I felt that I was treated unjustly, and this had to be addressed immediately. I went home, awaken my father out of his Saturday evening nap, and related the story to him. He asked me only one question: "Are you telling me the truth?"

"Yes," I replied. He then marched me back to the egg farm.

On our way, there was silence and each step seemed to only enrich the disposition of my father. I observed the determination on his face, and I felt somewhat afraid because my father, a black man, was going up against a white man. To question this white man just wasn't normal in rural South Carolina during the mid-1960s. But my father showed no signs of fear or intimidation.

We went directly to the owner's house and knocked on the front door. The owner came to the door. My father identified himself and forthrightly demanded the money that was due to me.

The owner refused. His reasoning was that I was the smallest of the crew, and he felt because of the size difference the larger guys should receive more pay.

That really agitated my father. The owner's justification was according to size? My father retorted with his own reasoning that was based on personal experience. He ended with another appeal for the money that was due to me.

Reluctantly, the owner reached into his pocket. But he paused to bring up the issue about size once again. My father paid no attention to the owner's unwillingness. The owner finally relented and gave me the two dollars.

I continued to work at the egg farm until I found other employment. But I never forgot about the stand my father made that day. The community received news of my father's actions with great jubilation. It seemed to have been a victory for them as well.

Will African-Americans ever get a fair shake?
We've been servants, now we need a break.
The corporate world, billions in the black,
We get less than, but nothing given back.

Why take measures to appear fair?
Everybody knows you've been caught in a snare.
Practices common in board rooms
Our presence, only when carrying a broom.

Multi-national company, global market,
Shot to the top of the news like a rocket.
The chairman directing spin control,
But nothing will change, so I've been told.

It must be a shame to be thought of as a bean.
Just think of the talk, most was really mean.
Big-time executives in the comfort of their space,
Their conversation and manners showed little taste.

Rev. Dr. Martin L. King, Jr.

A child reared in the southern way,
Earnestly partitioned for a better day.
Few willing to make his sacrifice,
For us he would pay the ultimate price.

He led the way, very humble,
While many around him started to crumble.
A spirit called to serve and save,
Could any one of us be as brave?

He would have loved to teach,
Touched by God, chose to preach.
He gathered all within his space,
We stood spellbound in his grace.

This graceful presence we miss—
The winds carry a solemn bliss.
Gone now, transcended to glory,
A committed life was his story!

Harriet

Could you imagine being hit in the head
For performing an act of mercy, being left for dead?
Through the pain and suffering, she hears a voice,
God wanted to use her; she had little choice.

Her stages of growth made it quite clear,
She had talents and gifts that were exceptionally rare.
Escape to freedom, shake loose those chains,
From that time forward she would never be the same.

Freedom, such a sweet taste to savor,
But commitment to her people, on this she couldn't waiver.
Bounty hunters, slave catchers and lots, lots more,
And to go back down South, a great risk for sure.

The release of hundreds of souls set free,
Her capture was never meant to be.
Moses, a parallel of a spiritual tone,
Thank God almighty Harriet was born!

Rosa

W eary, tired,
Seeking justice,
Thought of a less than,
Worked as hard as anyone can.

Quiet presence,
Soft spirit,
Inner strength willing to stand,
Not wanting to, but changing the land.

Jackie "50"

Baseball an American pastime,
But fifty years ago,
Few could cross the foul line.

Majestic forces stepped to the plate,
Initiating change,
Among all the hate.

This special man played the game,
Established a presence,
Handled the fame.

Many have come beyond that day,
The bases are now loaded,
Cause Jackie paved the way.

Dr. Carver

Traded for a horse, what a start.
No one thought he'd be smart.
A loner and inquisitive were his traits,
Never understood the reason for hate.

Searched for education as some the grail,
Refused to give up, refused to fail.
College opened its hallowed halls,
He ventured in; he answered the call.

Mr. Washington needed help on his quest.
He knew this would be the ultimate test.
Tuskegee Normal and Agricultural School,
Educate the "least among us" the only rule.

Research to aid the dispossessed.
Peanuts to reclaim the cotton's mess.
Life finally simple, a job and friend,
Service to humanity his only end.

Frederick Douglass

To grow up without a father or mother,
Little was known if he even had a brother.
Raised by a grandmother, shown lots of love,
Sent to nurture him from our Lord up above.

A spirit of unrest, grew deep inside,
Sent away to a breaker to adjust his pride.
Worked from sun up to sun down, pressured about,
Until the day he called the breaker out.

The constraints of a slave didn't fit him well,
The story of his life, to many he had to tell.
Freedom acquired through friends abroad,
Thanks to the blessing of our most gracious Lord.

One of many voices crying for justice,
While many in the South yelling, "Just trust us."
He stood tall, an intellect without measure,
His boldness for us we'll forever treasure.

Jack Arthur Johnson

At the turn of the century,
Jack was brave and quick.
Few could absorb his lick,
His swagger made whites sick.

Confident during a time people thought less,
Dialoguing with you without a care,
Whipping you with courageous flare—
Enter the ring if you dare.

A country not willing to change,
The country couldn't stand the heat,
Jack Arthur Johnson had to be beat
By the great white hope that'd be neat.

It's always nice to instill pride.
Colored people needed hope.
Jack Arthur Johnson pranced around the ropes,
Giving people the means to cope.

Buffalo Soldiers

W e never heard about you,
History reads a different way.
Did whatever task asked to do,
Braved the elements and Native Americans, too.

Native warriors coined the name,
Rode the range protecting the pioneers.
Wore the blue, performed the same,
Rustlers, outlaws, a land to tame.

Ninth and Tenth Calvary served us well,
Contributed to the nation's growth.
Helped win the west, many legends fell,
A story the west still longs to tell.

General Smalls

Born in a beautiful place,
Taken to Charleston,
Enslaved not free,
Hired out for a fee.

Pilot a steamship.
Engineer Brother John,
Experienced seaman and brave,
Never to remain a slave.

Escape a daring plan.
The confederacy secure and proud,
No one had a thought,
Freedom soon to be sought.

Actions mastered by clever stealth,
Sail away into freedom's light,
Determination and grit would prevail,
Hero and statesman, we proudly hail.

Tuskegee Airmen

You want to fly?
Come on, we'll give you a try.
Word given from the top,
Everyone expects a flop.

The Army Air Corp tried its best,
To put this notion to the test.
Demanding for the cream of the crop,
No room to fail nor even stop.

Hurry up with results,
The Negro will soon be out.
Tuskegee will only be a fling,
Flying is a white man's thing.

The news from Tuskegee is great,
God intervened; call it fate.
Not only did the Negro fly,
They excelled with only one try.

Mr. Robeson

Life spent breaking barriers,
Establishing truth.
It must have been tough,
Few whites cared for him much.

A voice of dignity and force,
Othello came to life.
Practicing lawyer, called to the stage,
A constant fight he had to wage.

Tall, proud, and confident,
Refused second anything.
Left, with great expectations,
To a country promising no limitations.

A life lived courageously,
Misunderstood by many.
Scholar, athlete, lawyer, performer, activist,
A great life we must insist.

Tarzan Would Never Do That

During the summer in Beaufort by the sea, we enjoyed long days and nights of afro-curling heat. The sun baked the ground to a sandy brown. Dogs would dig holes in the ground beneath the trees to cuddle and slumber. Our dog left holes of cool comfort throughout our yard trying to beat the heat. On many occasions, as my father cranked the car and began to move, our mutt would run from under the car yelling with tail tucked between his hind legs.

It was standard procedure during the summer never to wear your school clothes around the yard. All my friends dressed as I did in our Tarzan uniform. Tarzan was this white guy as far as we could see who was strong, brave, smart, and we sort of wanted to be like him. So, Tarzan was big among the simple country folks.

It must be established here that we only had a black-and-white television set, which only received five channels. Channels 4 and 5 were from Charleston; Channels 3 and 11 were out of Savannah, Georgia; Channel 7 was educational television. But I cannot remember seeing much of educational television unless it might have been on a clear night.

The rule in our house was simple when it came to the television. Whatever my father watched the rest of us watched. My father watched much television while he was sleeping; no one had the courage enough to change the channel.

Our Tarzan uniform was similar to that worn by the TV star with a little modification. In place of the loin cloth we wore an old pant cut above the knees and very tight. That was because as we grew the pant became tight and since it was summer there was no need for a fashion statement.

We would walk to our friend's house to play on the dirt roads The sand was cool to the bare feet. But there came a day when the powers-that-be paved our dirt road. Well, everything was fine until we ventured down the road barefoot on asphalt. We walked maybe ten steps before we realized that asphalt was much hotter than dirt. The asphalt burned the bottom of our feet. Every few steps, we had to soothe our feet in the dirt then resume our journey.

We were so caught up with Tarzan that we swung over a freshwater pond on vines behind our Aunt Marie's house. This particular pond we swung over was known to have an alligator in it. But we Tarzan wannabes; that didn't bother us. We got so good swinging over the pond that we would jump on the vine in groups of two just to force ourselves to go farther and farther as we felt the thrill of bravery and daring as our hero.

We told our Aunt Marie about the alligator and her eyes sparkled. Alligator, as I was to understand, tasted like chicken. So, she enlisted the help of Mr. John Hagman to acquire the alligator. He came by with his .22 rifle.

Mr. Hagman was an older man who lived alone but had the gift of fixing things. People brought their repairable items to him to fix at his leisure. You just didn't rush Mr. Hagman. His house was always filled with all types of things needing repair. He wore glasses, sported a white beard, and he had smooth brown skin—we kind of doubted that he was the man that could acquire the alligator for our aunt.

The alligator never came up that day, but the next day we went to the pond and spied on the alligator from the far bank. Mr. Hagman took aim and shot at the alligator. My brother, Leroy, Uncle Cladice, and I decided to go get him and carry him to our aunt. We got our red wagon and filled it with bricks, sticks, a pipe, and an ax to subdue our prey. (Keep in mind we had seen Tarzan do this many times on television, but without a wagon and supplies.)

We went down toward the egg farm road and into the bushes that surrounded the pond. We stepped over all kinds of debris before we cautiously approached the motionless reptile. His eyes were closed, but we were unsure if he was playing possum. So, we threw items from our red wagon to evoke movement. The bricks hit the tail, which moved slowly from side to side. We knew from Tarzan the tail was powerful, so we paid attention to its movement.

We got close enough to see blood coming from his head. We knew then that Mr. Hagman had wounded him. But we were still cautious. Our courage grew with each step to the point where we just pounced on him with everything we had in the wagon. We got the best of him in just a few minutes. Then we put him inside our red wagon and transported him to our aunt.

Mr. Hagman, being a jack of all trades, knew how to skin him. The tail was cut into small pieces by Aunt Marie, and it was put into a frying pan of hot grease until it turned brown. She brought the pieces to us in a pan, selecting to us portions to eat. We looked at each other, wondering who would be the first to taste the alligator tail.

Now, we had just seen Mr. Hagman skin him along with all the excitement of the catch. But to eat him just didn't seem right. Tarzan never ate the alligator he wrestled with on television.

With prodding from our aunt, we took a small piece, bit into it, chewed, and swallowed. It did taste like chicken, but we couldn't get the look of the alligator out of our mind. Tarzan would have never eaten the alligator, so us Tarzan wannabes should not have eaten it, either.

The Gullah culture, history and cute,
The indigenous people not making any loot.
Development springing up everywhere,
Dislocating the people without a care.

Collard Greens and Chicken

Well, there are some things you never outgrow,
Out achieve, never leave.
Turbulent and troubled, many want to forget,
Few allow that a bit.

Collard greens has sustained the slave, the maid
Beside macaroni it's laid.
Fried chicken that simple bird,
Stewed, baked,
Rotisseried, shaked.

Red meat is sin.
Veggies are in.
Fruit for dessert,
It's a shame words still hurt.

I'm Special

I must be important, can't you tell?
I demand you treat me well.
I'm arrogant, smart with lots of cash,
Get in my way I'm sure to mash.

You can't ever disregard my worth,
I've gained this through advent of my birth.
I live in a shallow world, gated and secure,
Most of my life is just a bore.

Soul Sockers

When I was about twelve, my uncle Butch started to play record hops at hole-in-the-walls. He called his group the Soul Sockers. His concept was playing music that was backed up by a live drummer. Most of the hole-in-the-walls relied on local disc jockeys to fill their establishments on weekends. The owners knew people got excited about the idea of record hops. Maybe it was because radio had conditioned them to embrace that type of entertainment.

Uncle Butch worked a regular job during the week, and he became Mr. Soul Socker on Friday and Saturday nights. Throughout the week, he advertised his next engagement by word of mouth, flyers, and the radio. He also purchased the latest records, which were usually 45s.

The business of record hops required a good drummer. Most of Uncle Butch's drummers were family and friends. My Uncle Cladice, who is Butch's brother, was his main drummer. The drummer kept the beat while the record played and the people danced. A good drummer could entertain the crowd just as well as the person on the microphone.

Uncle Butch was a showman on the mike. He invited the ladies to dance with him while talking on the mike at center stage (in front of the turntable and drums.) The crowd actually came to see their performance. The Soul Sockers had a reputation for packing the house. Besides uncle Butch and the drummer, there were individuals to guard the equipment and performers. He also traveled with about two carloads of people along with the groupies that followed him wherever he played.

Everyone dressed in the same type of tight shark skin pants that stopped just above the top of the shoe so the socks could be seen. They also wore some type of sweater or bly with a white T-shirt turned backwards to show the neck line. Their shoes were also shined—the Soul Sockers had a reputation to uphold.

In the club, most of us stood around the setup of a turntable and the drums. Most of the guys drank, so they had a brew in their hands looking cool. The main drink at the time was a Falstaff. I was too young to drink, but my uncle would give me small portions of a can to consume. That made me feel like one of the fellas.

Most clubs had beer licenses, but sold brown-bagged liquors illegally. So, liquor was usually served in cups poured from larger bottles. The members of the Soul Sockers brought their own drinks before going to the club.

Once the drinks mellowed out everyone, they zeroed in on the women. The Soul Sockers were also known for their dancing ability. The regular crew was a good-looking bunch of tall, charismatic men. Some of them were light-skinned. That mattered—keep in mind we're talking about being in the South—and the light-skinned brothers had it going on.

The basic dance at the time was the swing and the slow drag. The swing showed one's ability to be smooth and graceful on the floor. The slow drag, well, was just as the name identifies. Bodies were held tight together exploring erotic fantasies. The Dells hit song "Stay in My Corner" gave everyone a lot of time to explore.

Now that kind of environment was ripe for macho displays. The Soul Sockers could fight with the best any locale had to offer. Every community had a guy with a reputation for being the Man.

But there were ways around having to physically establish your presence. One of them was employing the Man to help collect money at the door, or maintain order in the club.

Yet when all of Uncle Butch's psychological maneuvering failed, one of the Soul Sockers would provide relief. On several occasions, different members of the Sockers proved their abilities extended beyond dressing, dancing, and drinking. Most of the fights were hand-to-hand and the party continued once it ended. Every so often, a gunshot would be heard, which cleared the club. But order was quickly re-established and the party continued.

One night as I stood in my usual spot next to the turntable and drums, a guy named Rod came up and told me that his girlfriend liked me and he was going to dismember my body parts. He was about twenty-five and I was fifteen. He was built like Hercules, and I was built like the guy who had the sand kicked in his face at the beach.

I knew the young lady in question, but I was innocent. I had not made any moves, although she did make some advances towards me. She was attractive and quite manipulative. She was dating him, but had let him go to seek opportunities elsewhere. I just happened to be caught in the middle being a new face in the crowd.

Well, the moment of truth arrived, Rod was set on keeping his promise. But one of the Soul Sockers came to my rescue. Cuda stepped in to defend his friend. I was one happy young man because I had no chance of victory.

Cuda told Rod to back off. He also said, "You will have to run through me to get to him." The fight started outside in front of the club. They wrestled and punched each other all over the ground. Between parked cars. Against trees. In and out of an encircled crowd.

In the end, Cuda was much quicker than Rod, which helped to neutralize his strength. He had carried the night, and I was one happy and relieved dude. We went back into the club and celebrated our victory. The young lady now socialized with us without any restraint. Rod even succumbed to the reality of their situation.

The hole-in-the-walls usually closed late into the morning. The group rapped up the equipment while Uncle Butch negotiated with the owner for payment. The crowd size was always the determining factor. The larger the crowd the more money was made. After paying the drummer, everything else was profit. Keeping the participants in the family also ensured a good profit.

Uncle Butch did well in the record hop business until he got the call from the Lord Almost overnight, he traded in his turntable for a bible. Nobody believed that he had made such a turnaround. Most of the fellas thought he was running some type of game until they saw him on Saturday mornings knocking on doors and preaching the good news of the Kingdom to whomever would listen

Come on, girl. Let's get close.
You know that's the place we love the most.
Our bodies touching, feel the thrill—
Together we explore every mountain and hill.

We dance as though we're one,
I can't think of any other way to have fun.
Sparks fly, we're generating heat—
You're my girl and very sweet.

Heels and Pants

Who invented heels and pants?
Give them a hand.
They have the thanks of every man.
A body prancing in a pair of pants,
Out of control we're in a trance.

Thanks, whomever it is to blame,
All pants don't wear the same.
Some are tight, some are loose,
But all carry a great caboose.
No mystery to this,
Girl, you give us fits.

It's My Right to Party
On a Saturday Night

Clean as Tide can get me
Out of the door, I'm gone
My lady is waiting all alone
Probably be early morning 'fo
We come back home.

Hit the club and buy a brew
Stand around scoping the place
Everyone cool showing lots of taste
Young ladies lovely the picture of grace.

The ladies add a mystic presence
Queen of the Egyptian Nile
Strutting with heels and style
Eyes glued on them all the while

The music gives a call response
Bodies flow to the rhythmic beat
Drinks release the freedom of fancy feet
Slow it down, it's been a long week.

Friday Evening Stop

After work with pay check in hand,
Done tired working all week for the man.
Get me to the bank, make it quick,
It'll be Monday 'fo I hit another lick.

On this paycheck, I sign my name,
Uncle Sam, off the top, just the same.
The rest is mine, give me cash,
Now to the liquor store I dash.

Get that half-pint, maybe a case,
Everyone ready to meet at my place.
We sneak a drink and pass it around,
We keep our eyes open as we pass thru town.

It's great fun to share a laugh and drink,
We pass some ladies, we give them a wink.
Our clothes are dirty; it's for sure,
But to hang with us is never a bore.

Most of my friends gather for fun,
We drink all our liquor 'fo it's done.
Before we split we make our plan,
It's sure great being 'way from the man!

Woman

Well, they're softer than we are,
Their bodies look better,
And they're soft to touch.
We love that very much.

When women speak,
Disarming, penetrating, chemical imbalance,
Something happens, who can tell?
Whatever it is, they're equipped quite well.

When they get close,
The heart begins to throb and pump,
Palms sweat, body changes, and watch out
Your inner being starts to shout.

Perfect, beautiful, an alarming presence,
A simple glance that certain thing,
Such power, loving, gentle, God knew best.
In their arms we long to rest.

Essence of Beauty

Brown sugar, caramel crème, chocolate almond,
Statuesque, natural beauty,
Such dignity, these women are proud,
Comfortable nobility, though never loud.

Rubies, diamonds, precious gems,
Silver and gold adorn their bodies.
Pearls only illuminate on black,
Sapphire gives a heart attack.

Pecan lovely, unforgettable style,
Chocolate almond, velvet soft,
Quiet strength, hypnotic allure,
Elegant presence, a woman for sure.

Brown sugar, silky smooth,
Caramel crème, seductive smile
Ebony princess, enduring grace,
Mother to the human race.

Memory

A song touches the heart,
It melts the most inner parts.
Just to listen takes you away
Into places felt in a special way.

Thoughts of that time of fun,
Lovers at the moment we begun.
Caress me and make me anew,
When I would say, "I love you."

Can I renew deep feelings of joy,
Make me once again your sacred toy.
Come to me as before,
Be mine forever more.

Trigger Bill

I used to hear my mother talk of an Uncle Walter, but I never saw him, not even a picture. He left home many years before I was born and it appeared that he never came to visit. Every now and then, a relative would mention Uncle Walter had been seen, but then he'd disappear again into his mysterious travels.

One day, I came home from work and Uncle Walter was sitting on the doorsteps with luggage and a big smile. He had paid an acquaintance to bring him home to Beaufort, South Carolina, his birthplace. He was eighty-three at the time and as physically fit as a fifty-year-old man. He was about five-five with broad shoulders and bowlegs. He had a head full of gray hair that only received Vitalis massages.

Uncle Walter had style. The family joked that he was kept alive by salt and alcohol—he liked to partake of the spirits. He smoked cigarettes and liked to joke around. He and I hit it off immediately. He called me "pepper head" and I kind of liked the name. He loved his family, especially my mother. My father took him as if he was a blood relative.

Now, Uncle Walter didn't have a place to stay so he stayed with us. He made his presence felt by helping with everything around the house. He was a great handyman and enjoyed company. But he was at a disadvantage when it came to conversations because his hearing was bad. We had to repeat things to him many times before he got it. We never paid much attention to this because we enjoyed being around him. He had a warm heart and sincerity that overshadowed any human frailties.

When he took baths, the bathroom would be full of steam. He liked his shower water hot. After his bath, he emerged from the bathroom in long drawers appearing like one of Santa's elves. He always dressed for warmth and comfort no matter what the weather was outside.

He'd sit at the table in the mornings drinking coffee and eating eggs, grits, and toast with such distinction. Legs crossed and enjoying the simple pleasure of a quiet moment with family. The television was on, but we knew he couldn't hear, although he was aware of it visually.

I drove a 1970 baby blue Ford Torino GT with a 351 Cleveland engine, jacked up in the back, and oversized tires. Uncle Walter loved to ride especially on the first of the month when his check arrived. He was generous with what he received. Gas and cold brew was a standard expectation whenever we went on these monthly cruises.

Uncle Walter told me a story of him once riding with his boss into town. The man refused to listen to anything he had to say, telling Uncle Walter to shut up whenever he tried talking. One day, they were parked and were about to get out of the vehicle when a car was coming toward them from behind. Uncle Walter recalled that he tried warning his boss about the oncoming car, but the man told him to shut up. The car rammed the door, taking it down the street. The driver never stopped. The boss cursed and yelled at Uncle Walter for the next week. The memory of the incident remained vivid with Uncle Walter as he laughed.

The first stop was always the bank. Uncle Walter couldn't read or write, so I acted as his representative. Uncle Walter had seen many things that I had only read about in this dual society of America. Beaufort of the early 1980s still embraced segregation and the ways of the Old South, but it had advanced beyond the time Uncle Walter left sixty years earlier. Nonetheless, he was quiet and reserved around white people. He observed his surroundings and measured his responses to fit the situation.

On this particular day, the line was long as usual and the tellers were short staffed. As we approached the next available teller, she put up a NEXT WINDOW sign. So, we waited our turn and moved to the next window to be served. That teller pointed to the man behind us to come forward.

I could not believe the blatant disregard for our presence. I appealed to the teller that we were next in line, but she was intent on holding her ground.

"The gentleman behind you had been waiting in line a long time and it's his turn," she said.

I replied, "He had just entered the bank. We were next and we're not moving."

Reluctantly, she relented, yet all the while repeating her position that the man behind us should have been served first. Uncle Walter never felt at ease in banks; I experienced first hand the discrimination that he had lived.

From the bank, we went to the nearest convenience store for refreshments. Uncle Walter had won the grand prize at the opening of a new store in our area: Two hundred dollars, ten dollars a week for the next twenty weeks.

Uncle Walter believed in carrying his gun with him wherever he went. He packed a .38. The gun itself didn't frighten me, but Uncle Walter with a gun was scary. He carried the gun loaded in his back between the waist of his pants and his spine.

He wasn't a good shot, either. He once tried shooting at a snake in the hollow of a tree, and he missed all six shots. Another time, he tried shooting a rabbit in our front yard. He missed again after several attempts. I finally shot the rabbit and we ate it that evening. After that, we nicknamed him Trigger Bill.

When Trigger Bill finally moved into a house of his own, nobody would venture up to his place for fear of being mistakenly shot.

Trigger Bill even bought himself a moped to cruise to the store. He was a sight to behold, riding on a red moped with goggles. His reflexes were slow, so that meant he fell a lot. He often came home dirty and bruised from his joy rides—he was close to ninety years old yet still going strong.

It seemed that Uncle Walter's health failed him almost overnight. One day, he was on the moped. The next day he was in a hospital bed. I was at his bedside at the end of his life. He was true to form even at the end; he once again disappeared into his mysterious travels.

I saw this black man,
With countenance bright,
He smiled at me,
Which made everything all right.
His smile radiated an inner peace,
Few words passed, to say the least.

Gone

Man, I used to walk this dirt road,
Went hunting over there in the woods.
Swam in the river, fished, too,
Now none of these things I can do.

Used to play sandlot ball in that field,
Some developer bought it at a steal.
Frolicked with my girl behind the big oak,
Few jobs, little money, now everybody's broke.

We would pile into one car,
Just to float and cruise
There were hangouts, places to go—
None are around here any mo'.

We enjoyed the simple life.
Nobody had much,
Friends were real.
Now, it's no big deal.

Lotto Fever

Lotto fever is what I've got,
Don't win but play a lot.
Some in church think it's sin.
But when I buy and maybe win,
All will claim to be my kin.

Heritage

The flag they wanted to erect,
Those groups a particular sect.
The hurt runs deep in some,
Molasses, slaves and rum.

Numba Two Tub

We're going to take a bath.
Hurry in, don't be last.
Rainwater in the tub,
We jump in and begin to scrub.

Mama done pour in Tide.
We begin to slip and slide.
Splash around, wrestle and fight
Get real clean fo' Saturday night.

Oh, the tub; oh, the tub,
Jump in and begin to rub.
The rainwater come from above,
Sent by God with his love.

Clean with a tint of ash.
Out of the tub we dash.
Run around naked and free,
Happy and clean as can be!

My Gifts

If I could paint like Michelangelo,
The prophets, the creation, an inspired man.
Just having one-tenth of his genius,
Wouldn't that be grand?

Maybe to stand for a cause,
Only believing it's right.
Like Nelson challenged superior forces,
Truth his army a determined fight.

Or to run a race like Jesse,
The world as his stage.
Taking on myths embedded,
Quieting all the rage.

Yet, just to be me,
The person I know best.
To develop and nurture my gifts,
That would be the test.

Acknowledgements

I thank God through His Son Jesus Christ for blessing me as a vehicle to display words that speak truth, love, and the humor of humanity. To God be the glory.

Secondly, I thank my parents for the courage they modeled throughout their lives. It constantly reassures me that I have nothing to complain about. Uncles Harold, Archie, and Walter would be proud

Finally, I thank the Heywards for your support—Vernelle, Monica, and Trey.

About the Author

Elijah Heyward, Jr. is a motivational speaker, public school teacher, businessman, and author. He lives in Beaufort, South Carolina, home of the Gullah culture.

His other published titles are *Shade: An Awakening; Hajile's Monster Guest; Hajile's Book of Riddles and Rhymes, Books I and II.*

Other Books from MavLit Publishing

Finding Your Virtue
Rodney B James
$9.95
ISBN-13: 978-1-9377050-0-8
Also available in ebook

Thoughts of Life: 360 E. May St.
B.H., Michigan
Birdman '313'
$14.95
ISBN-13: 978-1-9377050-4-6
Also available in ebook (Volumes I, II, III)

Husbands, Listen to Your Wives
Cedric Harmon
$11.95
ISBN-13: 978-1-9377050-2-2
Also available in ebook

www.maverick-books.com

36014519R00059

Made in the USA
Middletown, DE
22 October 2016